Come, Let Us Adore Him

John Sadler

ISBN 978-1-0980-1164-2 (paperback)
ISBN 978-1-0980-1165-9 (digital)

Christian Faith Publishing, Inc.
832 Park Avenue
Meadville, PA 16335
www.christianfaithpublishing.com

Printed in the United States of America

Introduction

"Our God is an awesome God.
He reigns from heaven above.
With wisdom, power, and love,
Our God is an awesome God."

This a song we sing in our church and it
rightly fits into this introduction. One day, the
Holy Spirit nudged me into writing the poems
that are in this book. I was wowed and came
closer to my Lord and Savior than I had been before.
When you start writing and sharing what God the
Father, God the Son, and God the Holy Spirit means
to you, it can only draw you closer. It has been
a blessed and sweet experience to share God's
awesomeness.

My prayer is that many will enhance their relationships with their
Mighty King who calls us friends. Also, that many will yield their lives
over to the one who loves us more than any other can.
We are to return the same to Him.

For His Increase!
John Sadler

Come Rhyme for Jesus

Who knows God knows what's in you
Long waiting to come out
The inward beauties He's woven
Tell the world what He's all about

In you, He's ordained and spoken
By His word which is your treasure
Is the power and will be your guide
And will be enough by any measure

To think you were a poet
And that you didn't know it
Just sit right down with pen in hand
And with Jesus, travel to your heartland.

It is His heartland now is yours
From forever was freely given
That living waters now to pour
On all who would surely listen

Try your hand at what can be
An opening of your heart and soul
As time goes on you'll realize
God's really got me on a roll

What you've put in me will come out
In ways I've never known
To touch someone, somewhere, somehow
To lead them to Your home.

Where he is, is everywhere
He's always here to give you help
Still giving of all that He can give
He knows we get worn out

He'll lift you up and nudge you on
You'll be different for the world to see
He says what's coming out of you
Is coming out for me

He's asking you to let Him in
For a journey that will be
A new excitement of joy and peace
And what's coming out of you
Is coming out for me

You'll be amazed and starstruck too
What you for Jesus can gather
There are those fields waiting for
The harvesters and He who matters

Inconceivable, Unbelievable

Inconceivable, unbelievable
That you would make your choice for me
For who am I but a lowly no one
A no one that's lived my life for me

That's all to change from this time on
I have brought you before the gang
To equip and empower you
By the power of my name

We have all been considering you
How to use you to bring to us
The souls of who we care about
So their souls would not be lost

I the Father, Spirit, and the Son
Are the gang, and we are one
To be your team to move you
For all our goals to be won

You don't have to figure anything out
You can leave that all to me
Faith in me is all you need
We will help you, you will see

By my Son, you have been bought
A price so great, you'll see
You can't do enough to pay me back
Your debt is covered by my mercy

You'll know your debt to me is paid
Has been paid and paid in full
When we open our gate and welcome you in
To comfort you and make you whole

And I have many miles to go
I'm running my race that will be won
I know when I cross the finish line
With the backing of the Father and the Son

To humbly stand in your presence
I've read how that may be
To see your glory and beauty
As for now, I can only imagine
But soon to see.

Our Mettle Detector, "Jesus"

Jesus, You see us as we travel
Upon this sphere made by You and God
You know our imperfections
Our lives, You're still working on

Parts of our lives that need to die
You helped to leave them in the dust
Your desire to create something beautiful
Something shiny that came from rust

We have been fading away
You caught us to make us new
From just a big lump of clay
To a treasure to glorify You

You are the Master Potter
Assuredly anything, You can create
Your children for the house of God
It is we You chose to make

As we live our daily lives
You tweak us from time to time
We are grateful to a loving Father
Who cares to keep moving us along

And what You're making is amazing
From one glory to another
Day to day as You check on us
We are different than most others

We are yielded and are willing
For You to check on what's our mettle
And it is a check on our own hearts
By the cross, a matter settled

You are the Master Mettle Detector
Ultimate authority for all our lives
What you see in us as our perfector
Is that You're the bond that ties

You tie us all together
In one big family
You've secured us so
That we won't roam
As we travel to
Our heavenly home.

What You See Is What You Get

Father, Your plan for us has been in Your plans
To touch our lives from before time began
For unto us, a child was given, unto us, a child was born
From this child, salvation will come
To encompass our entire world

How this Son of God and Son of Man
Would bring wonderment for all to see
Mary did you know His life was meant
To cover the sins of all humanity

As a baby in Your loving care
You hugged Him and kept Him close
Is this the little one You carried?
Is this the same Son upon this cross?

We thank You, Father, what we saw is what we got
And little Baby Jesus would someday suffer so
Forgiveness would be His last and forever stand
To release from the grip of death
Because of the sin of every man

Your servant, Simeon, had hoped to see
With Jesus's visit to the temple
He knew salvation to Israel has come
What he saw is what you gave
He went to rest in peace with that
Knowing You had blessed Him with what He got
King Jesus.

As Jesus Grew and Prospered
Blessed by Your presence and Your hand
All mankind will marvel
At what we saw is what we got

There are your years we know not of
As you grew in your family
You did Your work as a carpenter
It would affect every family tree

And as you used wood to build with
You knew to wood you would go
To intervene for my sins that are me
To be crucified upon a tree.

What we see is what we get
When to John, you came to complete
Fulfilling of all righteousness
The sign of a dove is what you set
Before all men to surely know

This is my Son in whom I'm well Pleased
Listen to Him in all He says
For I sent Him that you would be freed
From every sins to ruin you away

Where I want you to be
Do you want to be with me
To walk through heaven's door

And that sins grip on me
Would have no effect forever more?

When the enemy came to tempt you
With all the treasures of the world,
You did rise up and stand against him
By the power of your word

And then go forth with your power
To bring my lost sheep to me
For they will know and follow you
By the sign and wonders, they will see

When all the multitudes followed you
Saying if you are willing, you can heal
You saying, "I'm willing to whole be made
Leave all your excess baggage
Buried in the grave.

You can travel lighter
Be effective as my fighter
To spread my word everywhere
People will know you're different
And you care."

Souls that go from lost to saved
From lost to be upon my ship
And safe passage, I will give
Go and preach my gospel
That many souls will live.

You will see what I am giving
Is more than enough for you
You can be victorious
With all you say and do.

And remember how this started out
With what you see is what you get
We have miles to go to completion
And surely you're not done yet

I will touch many lives
As we travel upon this sod
With miracles, signs, and wonders
Everyone will know that I am God

Without me, you are nothing
With me, you are everything
And the mountains you need to move
You'll move them because of me.

I am a God of love and hope
My son is a gift from me
To fill your lives with what I gave
What I gave was to see you free.

There are so many wonders
That I have seen from you
And reinforce my commitment
To press onward till the end.

You are the real deal for me, dear Lord
Not knowing why You would deal for me
Your love has covered all my time
My times needed what You gave.

You would leave your family
To travel upon the roads
And secure your Father's history
With the saving of men's souls.

When it was time for you to get here,
You didn't have to travel very far
To find the men by the sea
To support the work of the Savior
Who is my God and King

And off, you all would go
To perform miracles men would see
How many thousands that you touched
To make soldiers for the cross

From victory unto victory,
We are on the winning team
To love and serve our Savior
Full service to Him is what He means.

Your chosen disciples' feet, You washed
To be an example of how we're to be
To be a servant of all mankind
To draw all people unto me

What we get from what we see
The bloody brutality even before the tree
By Your love, You would be crucified
Throughout the world magnified

I sit here to contemplate
The ending of this prose
You have your own ideas
In continuing about the cure
For all mankind's woes

I will move to end this narrative
You have more riches for me to share
Your Holy Spirit and Helper
Is guiding to show you care

I look forward in anticipation
What your spirit cares to share
It will be good and the culmination
Of the victory for men everywhere

The journey of this writing
You have blessed me to share
I can't thank you enough, but I'll try
To serve you and exalt you
As you give me breadth to dare.

Love Is the Key

John 3:16

Jesus, surely You hold all the keys
To unlock hearts won for You
And have sent Your spirit to seal
The hearts and make known what to do.

Faithfully You lead and direct
By the power and might of Your word
The wiles of the enemy brought to nothing
With ammunition, that is Your sword

As a gentle shepherd, You search
For the lost sheep seeking
To bring them safe and sound
One of Your lost sheep was me

Dear Lord, there are many hearts broken
That are in need of Your mending
You tell everyone there's no pretending
Because You gave all to bring all

I know you left nothing on the table
All that follow need to do the same
You gave all and ask nothing less
All Your children take on your name.

For the name of Jesus, we travel
Sprinkling the crumbs of Your love
When followed leads to Your home
The followers will find love from above

Jesus has the key to your heart's lock
His unlocking for to set you free
And go into the world for Him
Showing your love and service for me

He stands as a proud father
As proud as can be
Knowing what He's done and accomplished
To make us free to love and to see.

We have made the right choice
In receiving the love for Jesus
There's nothing more in the universe for me
Than to have and share His love eternally.

The Next Step Is Heaven

We have many steps in life that we are made to take
From inception to perfection and all that comes before the end
And Jesus molding as a potter from a wretch to a saint to make
That we, His children, are not anxious before it's time to send us
To the Father and the Son and for their glory to be revealed
And by His Holy Spirit, we are wondrously and marvelously sealed

Could anyone have imagined that God could love someone like me?
But that's the step He took not something I could foresee
He foreknew and planned to accomplish His will
And regardless of my shortfalls, He loves me and loves me still
"Why me?" I asked, and no answer was ever given
But He's guarded me in letting me know, the next step is heaven.

How many steps I've taken that to Him was all so wrong
He patiently and lovingly has kept moving me along
Until that day, I stand before Jesus to be judged
And He puts his arms around me, and I know that I've been hugged
By my Lord and Savior and from Him He calls me friend.

Of all the steps that we can take to see where we are going
Is the one that is most important to see what Jesus is doing
He came in love and lived in love to show us how to live
And died in love to accomplish the Father's will
What a father, what a son that we are forgiven

To pay what we owe can never be fathomed or imagined
Because it is so great a sum that Jesus paid for us
What more could we do for Jesus, our precious Savior

Than to give our all and be all in until we go back to dust
And now we are ever closer to our salvation
Than when we first believed
Can you imagine? Can you believe what Jesus has done for me?
Hallelujah! Hallelujah! The next step is heaven.

I Am Willing

Luke 5:12–13

To those of us who are like those of us
We are all bundled in life together
Are all sinners in need of Christ's great love?
So we can experience life's better weather.

Jesus has His eyes on us and wants us to succeed
To be more than conquerors because of Him who loves us
And we can get inside the ship that will sail us to safe waters
For He is willing, and He is able, for Jesus is who that matters.

I must decrease, and He must increase is what I really want
He will mold and make me in who I need to be
To glorify the Father and the Son forever in eternity
Jesus says, "I am willing," for us to see what He wants us to see.

When we knock upon His door, He lovingly will open
Invite us in to learn of Him to all who are so broken
Jesus will lift us up and heal all that does need, healed,
We can go into the world with Jesus to us revealed

To show how great a Savior has entered into our lives
He wants to be your Savior, to you and yours tonight
His great love knows no bounds; He wants for you to know
When you reach out and call to Him,
He'll be right there for to show "He is willing."

The Shepherd and the Lamb

Dear Lord, it's hard to think of you
As the shepherd and also the lamb
You came down to lead your sheep
To guide us to your Promised Land

You also came down for your Father
To be his sacrificial lamb
For your blood to cover all of us
In the end we'd not be damned

As a faithful shepherd
Caring always for your sheep
Constantly watering and feeding
Our feelings for you run deep

At the start of your ministry
You knew where you were heading
Many signs and wonders that you did
It started at your friends wedding

Your signs and wonders continued
You had an army that was renewed
Your presence both then and now
We're renewed by your somehow

We say somehow for we don't know
Our trust is forever in you
What you do, you do for us
It's what no one else can do

As your sheep we wander
Always looking for better pasture
We need your wisdom and your concern
As for sheep and people, it's hard to learn

What is good for sheep is green pasture
What is good for people is a faithful pastor
To speak the truth, the truth with love
To keep us safe and avoid disaster

For there is a wolf just waiting for
A victim to go astray
And our faithful shepherd
His presence will keep him away

What dangers that we do not see
Our shepherd has always known
As sheep we seek your comfort
As people we seek a crown

A crown is what comes from you
As you welcome us to your home
With words, "Well done good and faithful servant
Your work on earth is done

And I see you as my Savior
Hanging there upon the cross
As long as you had breadth in you
Your family would have no loss

Even in your weakened state
You had strength for all to see
Forever you are the mighty king
You forgave us and set us free

What you did and what you saw
With your last breath's at Calvary
To look upon your mournful mother
As for a Son she'd have another

All the events at your cross
As far as time would not take long
You would leave from this old world
And not really would you be gone

After being taken from the cross
In three days your presence came
All would see our Jesus and Savior
That you had taken all our blame

For a perverse and wicked generation
And all generations for to come
You for knew and you for saw
The victories that would be won

As you transformed and conformed
From the cross to a rightful king
To love and lead your followers
To something beautiful they hadn't seen

Your majesty before not seen
We see you as in a dream
Oh no! It's not a dream
It's our Savior, God and King

He's standing there to nudge you
To step across the finish line
To come through the narrow gate
Don't you worry, you won't be late

We can see all our family ones
From up here down to there
In that dimension a great gulf is fixed
The dimension that we came from

We have joy and peace to share
Our worries they are none
Praise and worship of our king
Is the main reason why we come

One last thought I care to share
When on earth I cried for you
Because you first cried for me
And now I know I was supposed to

If your savior means so much
Means so much to you
If you want to cry for him
Do it now, for in heaven it won't be allowed.

Our Hope and Faith

2 Corinthians 4–16

Therefore, we do not lose heart
We've been made a part of God's family
We know our outward man is fading
Our bodies moving onward are waning
He is with us.

He is with us to renew our mind and spirit
Jesus will ever guide and lead us
Empowered from His power from on high
That when we leave, we don't die
We've been reprieved.

While we're here to love and serve
To speak for God's goodness to all who'll hear
Since we are here and not gone yet.
To be fishers of men for God's love net
Fish away.

We look forward for all that's in Your Word
And mighty than mightier is Your sword
We can be more than conquerors
With all the armor You have given
Fight away.

When our time on this earth is done
The gift of eternal life is won
Where could we have gone without Jesus?
Our Lord, King, and Master who calls us friend
This is not the end.

Who's "Wooing" You?

In this world, there are distractions
Wooing you to show reactions
To pull you away from who really counts
How much to you does he amount.

His blood, the cross, His love, His loss
Jesus is wooing you
My sin washed clean at what a cost
Jesus is loving me.

What a light coming from the dark
From the dark to the light to see
I'm so thankful and so grateful
That Jesus is wooing me.

Just one taste of His heavenly realm
A realm I'll strive to see
If it's a taste, I'll cling to
For Jesus to keep wooing me.

He sets us apart to show the World
How caring He and His Father can be
He's filled my life with love and joy
I know who's wooing me

So ask yourself, do I have a plan?
To fight the evil confronting me
For of myself, I have no strength
Thank God, Jesus is wooing me.

He keeps me close as close can be
He sees so much more than I can see
Of all that can befall His saints,
Jesus is wooing me.

So who's wooing you? Who's wooing you?
Remember there's the world against us
We're still suffering from the fall.

So who's wooing you? Who's wooing you?
There's so much that God has given
To secure you in His fold.

From sinners to the winners
And from ain'ts to the saints
And the question, God does ask
Who's wooing you?

Reign Us In

O Lord, we are so lost
That ever our needs for You
You've bought us and have saved us
And what a sacrificial cost.

Jesus, You know how we are
Because You came to live with us
It's amazing that our stench
Wasn't something that drove You off.

Your love and sacrifice for us
Is how Your life was fashioned
Although Your gift is undeserved
It was because of Your compassion
Reign us in.

We are grateful and thankful
That Your desire is to be with us
And we can be so thoughtless
How we live to show just such
Reign us in.

Help us to be more mindful
Of Your being with us all the time
That we can be more timeful
Of the time we give to You
Reign us in.
Lord Jesus, reign us in.

Christs Love

Love of love and love of life
We experience because of His sacrifice
To really and really and really know
The ultimate and real love He came to show

That now and forever, we have
The greatest of the gifts to make
A better world for all to see
That His love is the purest that can be.

And with this love, mountains can be moved
To make a difference in broken lives
And all honor and glory for His sacrifice
To make us new.

Can this love really make us new
To be a beloved servant of our Lord
That we can really cut the cords
Of our old lives?

To forget and remember no more
Of who we were and what we did
Before Jesus in love opened the door
And let us in.

That we have become saints, indeed,
His love has pushed us forward
To run the race, He has ordained
We are forever moving forward.

We can know, and we can know
That Jesus is ever for us
And we can know, and we can know
He's always ever in us.

Just in Time: The Roaring Lion

Lord, I think how dear You are
How dear You are to me
I think of many days gone by
And the subtleness of my enemy
When he thought he had me
And to heaven, I wouldn't fly
You stepped in and intervened
And to heaven, I will go by and by
You have all the bases covered
To keep me safe and reel Him in
Stupid of him not knowing
I've always been in Your hands.

And so the lion found me
When I was weak and couldn't stand,
Just in time, You saved me
I was protected by Your command
To me, You said, "I have this."
To Satan, you can have none of him
For he was lost and now is saved"
Is in my family and in my hands
We have done all what it takes
To keep Him in our fold
We have set our eyes on Him
Part of the greatest story ever told.

What's in my word will protect Him.
And what's in my word will direct Him
To be my servant and my child

To have more joy than he can hold
I have set in motion, my servant David
Mr. Wilkerson of World Challenge
To send a word from me was given
To set a captive free.

Your prophet and friend, Isaiah
In chapter 41, did say,
"Fear not for I am with you"
I am with you this very day
My right hand will hold you up
And those that war against you
Shall be told to "shut up"
They shall be nothing in the end.

By Your word, You saved me
My life was speeding by
And just how fast You caught me
In the twinkling of an eye
To halt the one who would destroy
To take me to His cavern
Oh no, you can have none of me
For my home is with God in heaven
And You've always been just in time
Always just in time for me
When I get with You in heaven,
It will be my time to just begin.

Your Angels

How You use Your angels
Totally dedicated to You
To step across the line
To intervene in our lives

You know and see a need
To dispatch one of Your blessed angels
To serve behind the scene for You
And win battles we never see.

Angels are at Your disposal
Because of Your love for us
To mix it up, come out on top
Put the enemy in retreat

There are those times we realize
Something special has just happened
With the pulling of our heart strings
And Your angel has been realized.

To test in us our love for You
Did we pass the test?
And did we do our best?
To be followers of our King?

Your teachings of compassion
The fruits You want to see in us
For us to reach out as You would
To show the greatest gift is love

The presence of Your angels
Is too often that we miss
They are here and gone and nowhere
Disappear as in a mist.

And we know that in our spirit
You have sent a help to us
Your help is stirring our spirit
To bring us closer to our God

Do we learn when we pass the test?
And do we learn when we fail?
Your patience that You show to us
Encourages us to prevail.

I wonder when we come to You
What duties are given to us?
Will we be sent to serve You?
As angels unbeknownst.

A Bout with Doubt

To all My children
That I care so much about
Although I'm humble and loving
I am also still a King.

The authority I've been given
To watch over and care for you
You can be founded in My word
And have no bout with doubt.

Consider Me strong and doubtless
All My words will smother you
To be secure and never wavering
For all My promises that I will do

When I promise, it's a promise
That I will always bring to pass
There can be nothing in this universe
Can stop My words, forever they will last.

Be secure in Me, your King
I'll lift you up to walk with Me
You're of Me, a royal priesthood
You can marvel of our victory.

Love-Driven, His Gift Given, My Testimony

John 3:16

Just how much You loved me
On that very special day
When You came into my life
And my sins were wiped away

Why You ever chose me
I don't know, and I may never
It's enough to know that I am here
To be with You forever.

What a time and what a place
That You graciously did choose
To reach to where I was
And where I was, was far from You.

When Your Holy Spirit spoke
And said it's "now or never."
With fear and chills, I'd never known
It's the way that You that You were given
I knew it was a gift from God
And that it was love-driven.

To change in me Your change for me
With confidence, I can go forth
To shout it from the housetops
How much my Savior's worth.

To give to Him forever

All there is in me to give
Would I have made things different?
My answer is "no, never."

I will be amazed and comforted to see
All my saintly family
That have been waiting patiently
And I can say, "Look, it's really me."

To share new life with all who come
With all who come to see
What a Father and a Savior
And with a promise He's given me.
All that I could hope for
No longer is it withheld
To know the things, I never knew
And Jesus says, "It's okay, and that it is well."

So when it's time for this life's ending
It will be time for new beginnings
I can only imagine the new life that will be
With his angels, Father, Son and me.

Skedaddle

Skedaddle means to get away fast
If that word gets into your head
It's in there, and it will last
To be a part of your speech forever

Jesus had to skedaddle on many occasions
To separate from the people to rest
When they found Him, there was a people invasion
And Jesus and His men were put to the test.

His compassion for the lost was Him
He could not, not take care of them
However tuckered out He was
He was their shepherd and took them in.

There were times when He would fast depart
From those who would do Him harm
They would see Him, and He'd be gone
And they placed their rocks back on the ground.

His time to go had not arrived
His time to gather people to Him
He would not leave before His time
Shortly He would die and then be alive.

Did Jesus skedaddle with His men
When in the garden, it was time
For Him to be taken and not given back
The leaders charging Him with a crime?

Will Jesus have to rush when in heaven?
After the cross, He's our Almighty King
Being judged and being forgiven
Tenderly brought alongside of Him.

Jesus is on the throne, and He is different
Time means nothing more to Him
His skedaddle days are over
He's at heaven's door to welcome us in.

Our skedaddle days are still here
Whatever we do, we need to do this
To skedaddle to our Savior's arms
To be welcomed with a holy kiss.

When we are in heaven, I wonder
What our time and regimen will be
To honor and glorify our loving Savior
Skedaddle will have no part of me.

Going Off the Deep End, Getting on the High End

How in life our letdowns are many
As pressures increase, we sometimes say,
"Is there any help for me? Is there any?"
To lift me up from the mire I'm in daily.

As people notice all our struggles,
There is a saying, "Going off the deep end."
It's the place we happen to be,
And we're open for the world to see.

But there is someone we can turn to
Who is above all creation, and that is we
He can turn all our situations around,
And God is for us and wants us to see.

There is nothing our God can't do
Be heartened, His love will show
That he's putting us on the high end
Because He considers us more than a friend
Thank you for the many messages you send.

My Realness for Your Wellness

From the beginning of My creation,
I saw everything I created was good.
If you haven't notice what I did,
It's high time to know you should.

I created the world for all your good
To acknowledge and give Me credit
I am a jealous God, and you should know
I want good for you and not call you wretched.

My realness you need to know about me
Having faith in Me, you'll see a wellness
For I watch over all My saints
I am Almighty God, please show a stillness

When you stop to think about Me
You'll know I'm right beside of you
To give you hope in life, leading
A light you'll have by My word's reading.

You'll see, I keep My children well
Telling them to go and speak about Me
Pulling them away from the enemy's hands
For freedom proclaimed throughout the land.

To be set free as part of your wellness
You're free to worship and serve Me
To honor and glorify My swellness
And see me as swell to all your needs.

Seeing My realness for all your cares
I'll never leave you or forsake you ever
What a guarantee I do give
Whether it's calm or stormy weather.

You can come to Me whenever you need
I care enough to be there for you
I ask do you care enough for me
To be obedient in whatever you do.

I gave my Son to make you well
You not knowing you were something less
Not well at all but really sick
And most your life has been in distress.

He's the perfect shepherd for you to follow
So get on board and join us now
Most assuredly don't delay until tomorrow
Experience us for your moment to be wow.

Wow, moments will draw you close to me
And intimate times will soon follow
Open your heart for us to enter in
You'll know our realness because you allowed

Us to enter in and make you well
For you to exclaim it is well with my soul
Your realness to me you have showed
All of me and what I have owed.

To my Almighty God and Savior
Never can I give enough
For you were all in, all in for me
Praise you, Lord, you've allowed me to see

What your realness has to do with my wellness
It's your loving gift you've given me
Is there anything more real than my King?
The real truth and answer is nothing.

Our full wellness, we won't experience
Until in heaven with our great King
All the promises you have delivered
Have come to pass, and they are remembered.

Jesus Is on the Way

To all who think that life just sucks
Hopes and wishes are never to fill my day
Be informed that it's not so
Jesus is on the way.

He's done all for what it takes
To bring you close to Him
For you to know and believe
That Jesus is on the way.

He's forever always near you
And wants you to be His
What more can He do than He has done?
So secure your life with Him.

For what a great transition
To go from what I was to what I am
And it's all because of Jesus
His great love has brought me in.

To a family that is forever
And forever I'll be known
As a child of God who wishes
To make my abode in my real home

Jesus came and met me
And wants all to Him to come
And remember the days from the past
And what you have and have come from

That to think Jesus has been on the way
To get to me from there to here
How foolish and not knowing
He always has been near.

What's in A Name

A common saying that is glossed over
What's in a name
There is a name means more than any other
He holds existence in His hands

With the angel Gabriel's visit
He would set events in motion
That would affect all mankind
From nation to nation

The name of Jesus
From God the Father
For Gabriel to deliver
To Mary His blessed Mother.

A gift to the maid servant
Of the Lord God Almighty
For all mankind to be touched
Mary did you know that Jesus
To so many would mean so much.

And what's in a name
A name whose kingdom
Shall have no end
And those that come to Jesus
Will be born for their lives to begin.

The mighty name of Jesus
The loving name of Jesus
How much can be in Your name?
You graciously let us share the much
As Your family glories in Your fame.

Our allegiance is to our Savior
Whose name is higher than any other
We will learn of why
To not let Jesus pass us by.

Your name is what we cling to
The name of Jesus, a beautiful name
How you let us know about you
And all the reasons why you came.

What's in the name of Jesus?
That a captive would be set free
With a freedom to go into the world
A witness for all the world to see.

Look upon His beauty, and His always caring
For the sheep of His pastures
And our souls, He is comparing
To His love standard, if you love me

Feed my sheep
What's in your name that guides you
To be about your Father's business
The Father's love for you from Him
And yours to Him is the victory for all men.

Many battles, we'll battle to be won
Our confidence is in our Lord
Jesus, the Father's only Son
That's always moving us along

And what's in a name?
Reach out to Jesus, and you will see
He'll reveal himself to you
To see His Majesty

For if He is all in for you,
You'll realize there's a time
For you to be all in for Him
Thank you, Father, what a find.

But you first found us
Not a lovely find for you
You would tweak and refines us
To completely make us new.

I hope the world can see
How great a name can be
Jesus, Your name is above all names
Is above all names to me
What's in a name!

His Cross Will Lead Us Home

Dear Lord,
Before You went upon the cross?
Thousands upon thousands did follow You
They yielded to You to be their boss.

They saw in You a greatness
A kind and loving shepherd too
That would care for His flock no matter
Whatever dangers would ensue.

If God is with You and for You
Who would dare to come against
Our great God of love and compassion
For all mankind, by God was sent.

To all the many, whoevers
Would give their lives for Christ
Will have a true path to follow
As it leads them to the cross.

To follow you to your somewhere
We have a Son to lead us on
Father, thank You for our Savior
By the cross, our victory won.

From the cross, we'll travel on
To wherever the Spirit leads
Knowing every step we take
Leads to where our souls will meet.

To Your cross and from Your cross
There are many stories to be told
You have captured the souls for you
More precious than fine gold

How my cross has captured you
To draw you close and send you away
To go and do your work for me
And for sin to have no sway

You are free to go and do all things
Do all things in My name
The things never seen before
You are My miracles on display

Go from My cross into the world
And know My spirit is within you
Many lives gained for My kingdom
My cross will lead you home.

"You"

The fame of your name will ever last
Through Eons and millenniums
Your blood on the cross covers my past
As I move on in my continuings.

What's in store for me tomorrow?
I don't know and will find out
Perhaps joy or laughter or sorrow
It's what life is all about

There's a different life that's your life
To us, you so freely expressed
For us to have and be grateful
As we move closer to your rest.

It is a rest we can count on
When our time down here is done
But for now, we'll serve you here
With joy, peace, and comfort won

Come to me, You who labor
You will find rest unto your souls
For great is My love for you
And I am God and in control.

Put Me in your daily lives
See My glory and presence revealed
All your hurt and cries and pains
Given to Me, they will be healed.

If you decide to stand by Me
Most assuredly, I'll stand by you
As a mother hen to protect her chicks
From all that can come against.

Know that I'm God, and for you,
My intentions are for you to succeed
Remember My apostles and servants
Were in prison, and by Me, were freed.

An angel from Me was dispatched
To give instruction to My beloved
To stand and speak within My house
The words of this life I've given.

Take My words into the world
No partiality will I show
Salvation can be done and not just for some
I'm willing that all will come.

Well done, My faithful servant
You will hear Me before you stand
Before My throne and judgment seat
What a difference My words have made.

The Sooner, the Better

The sooner the better, a term we hear often
A saying we should adhere to, surely before the coffin
When Jesus came to lead all men to Him
Many never realize, He's the only way to win.

The sooner we come to know Him
The better for many to come in
Into His house and into His family
A safer boundary than anything.

The many years that I was lost
The opportunities that swept right by
Souls that never heard from me
If I was sooner, I could have testified

It would have been better if I was sooner
And had more time to speak of Him
Many lost sheep of many pastures
Could have been forgiven of their sins.

Will this sin of my omission
Be weighed and judged to my account?
Will Jesus love and forgive me
To pick me up and let me count?

Should my life to me be a lesson?
There's no time to waste anymore
For the fields are white to harvest
The end of time is knocking at the door.

It's time to harvest the good fruit
That's been planned before time began
The good fruit will bless us all
The bad will be squashed in the fall.

God's ways are far above our ways
His grace and mercy are up there too
His love for those we never thought
Had a chance, and God came through

And those who we always thought
Would be the ones to be in heaven
A complete surprise would be to us all
Have been judged and thrown out with the leaven.

Christ has said not everyone
That says Lord will enter in
But those that do My will
Will see My open arms and My grin

Jesus is happy to welcome us
To His kingdom known as the by and by
And who knows that some of us
Will have wings and able to fly.

And all of this takes the back seat
Why to heaven and heaven, we came
To thank and praise our God and King
For all of everything that He gave.

To make of us His sons and daughters
To worship Him without regret
For He is worthy, and He is great
Has turned us all into His saintly saints.

To know of all His kingdom's gifts
And coming from there to here
Knowing that the sooner we came
For the better, we'd never be the same.

Gone Fishing

The many times I've gone fishing
I came up short with no fish to bring
The bait that I was using
Was not the bait that was their thing.

I came home dismayed and dejected
I had no fish for us to have
As for the Lord, the fish He wants
Are the ones for Him we are cast.

We are cast into the world
His word to us is to go
Go and catch souls for me
And to sit down at His love feast.

When Peter said, "I go-a-fishing,"
Other disciples said, "We go too,"
Not knowing the risen Savior
Was there to see them through.

He came to the edge of the sea
The men not knowing it was He
He asked, "Have you any fish?"
The disciples claimed, "We wish."

He said, "Cast your net to the right,"
They would catch so many fish
It was so easy without a fight
So many fish in so little time, what a sight

Jesus wants us to cast our nets
To go fishing just for Him
And the fish that we will catch
Are His ones, so reel them in.

When leaving to go fishing
The Lord is going with us too.
The bait that the Lord will give
Will catch to be thrown back to live.

His words, they are mighty
To the tearing down of every throne
For His words are life everlasting
To bring in all to one big home.

To everyone, His words go forth
Go and catch many souls for Me
I have made you fishers of men
My earthly ministry began at the sea.
To catch the disciples that I would need
To be mighty people, mighty for me
And now to everyone of mine
Catch some fish and set them free.

Plum Tuckered Out

Lord, as You were growing up
Working as a carpenter with Your father and brothers
Even when Your days were long
It would be nothing like what would be Your others.

Other days would come and go
Your life would be hitting the ground running
Watching over Your disciples and followers
And their daily needs, it was quite stunning

There were constant needs that would go on
For three years, the needs would always be
Even up until You were gone
And came back to cook breakfast by the sea.

As You traveled and miracles done
Word would go out across the countryside
Throngs and multitudes would flock to You
For healings and demon dealings
For You to be lifted higher.

Your fame was like a brushfire
The wind of the Holy Spirit keeping
Your name daily on the tongues of men
For Your purposes the harvest reaping.

When the thousands came to You
Hurriedly coming because word of You
Was traveling throughout the heartland
For the capturing of people's hearts

Your love and Your compassion
For the sheep that were so lost
Moved You forward and moved You on
To where tiredness was here and gone.

As a mortal, You would need
Sleep and rest to restart
Another day much the same
Fame of Your name is why they came.

To come to a shepherd that is so caring
All the sheep's needs were always met
Your disciples came to be fishers of men
And many were caught in Your love net.

Lord, You would have to depart from them
To recharge Your human traits
To spend time with Your Father in prayer
Knowing His purposes for You were right.

Another day would come and go
Very much as the day before
In You, knowing why You came
For the masses to enter Your door.

Day in and day out is what You're about
Always giving of Your loving self
It's no wonder You were always
Plum tuckered out.

In Your place, on heaven's throne
All seeing and knowing people's hearts
That we can come whenever to You
You're always and ever there for us
And never tuckered out.

Sunset, Sunrise, Sunset, Christ's Last Day

Jesus, as Your time drew near
Having Passover with Your disciples so dear
Minus one.
The Last Supper that was started
The days ahead were for us
To remember You so dearly departed
From the Passover to the Last Supper
Both to glorify Him of our hope
How our Lord and His presence
Protects and lifts us for to cope.

When Your time in the garden had come
You with Your disciples were there
Of those that You gave me, I lost none
Even though in time they would run.

The betrayal that Judas would enact
Multitudes with him came
Peter rising with the sword he had
And one ear of an enemy dispatched.

Jesus to Malchus, "It will be all right."
Your ear will be back for all to see
Even with My miracle done
Will you not turn to believe in Me?

Earlier when you made your approach
That Jesus, you were here to seek
Me telling you, "That it's me you need"
Then you all fell to your knees
Something must have told you I am a King.

To Caiaphas, you would escort me there
Him saying there should be one to bear
The misdeeds that are noticed by Rome
And there should be none to claim a throne

When questioned by Israel's High Priest,
Your betrayer, there in the mix
His questions of your disciples and doctrines
Not knowing you were sent to be the world's fix.

The ignorance of the High Priest's officer
In not knowing who He was striking
The King of Kings and Lord of Lords
Someday He would stand before Christ's court.

To the courtyard, Peter had come
Jesus had extolled Peter as the one
"Upon this rock I will build My church
And the gates of hell shall not prevail."

When questioned by a servant girl
As a disciple of Jesus, he said, "I am not."
As Peter warmed himself with them
Now knowing He was part of a prophesied plot.

Two more times, he would deny
Being a disciple of Jesus His King
The last time by a relative of Malchus
Whose ear had been healed by Him

Off to Pilate, they would lead the King
To cast judgment because Israel's rulers couldn't
Pilate's wife warning not to bring
As for as judgment on Him, you shouldn't.

Pilate sought to release Jesus to them
The people cried out more
Let Jesus be crucified and from Him
He's claimed to be a King against Caesar.

Pilate to the people, "I find no fault in Him."
The Jews saying, "We have no king of our own men,"
The leaders led Him away and broke their own law
To put to death the one God's prophesy foresaw.

To die for all that some may live
To stand before our King
To be welcomed in and comfort found
For our new lives to begin.

Before that, Christ would suffer much
To be beaten and abused
Then to be placed upon the cross
The cross Simon would carry for Him.

Traveling to Golgotha, they would arrive
After the abuse, Jesus was still alive
To fulfill the wishes of His Father
The cup I must drink is for no other

The nails that went in His hands and feet
To secure Him to the cross for all to see
Mary, his mother, would become undone
To see the suffering of Jesus, her Son.

Barabas would see where he should be
Not among the people who were free
That all of prophesy would be fulfilled
On this day that God has willed.

Jesus, our King, would express to some
His mother and loving disciple John
And to the thief upon the cross
"This day in paradise with Me, you'll be"

The pain and agony our King took on
That we the guilty of our sins
To be set free, His victory won
It's been accomplished by God's only Son.

When Jesus our King took His last breath
It was our sins that put Him to death
The many soldiers marveled to see
The graves opened the saints set free.

The earth shook, and the rocks were split
A centurion seeing all that was before Him
And surely, He knew who was the cause
Saying truly the Son of God He was.

Joseph of Arimethia came
And to Pilate made His request
To take the body of his loving King
To His own tomb, put him to rest.

All of what the hours had told
That our King was walking the streets of gold
And from there to here, earth to come
To still guide and lead the some.

Forty days, You would show Yourself
To the five hundred picked by You
Your longing to secure Your people
Made it hard for You to go.

And finally, You left us
To go to the Father above
Who had blessed You
With the sending of the dove.

The promise of the helper
To live in us and to show
Your love for the whole wide world
Would cause a forever light to glow.

The Virtuous Wife

What a treasure one man may find
The gift of a wife by one divine
She wishes and desires a family
Not only a wife but a mother to be.

She has a love and relationship
Far greater than humanly achieved
To be part of her heavenly family
Jesus says, "Come in and dine with me."

By her having her priorities right
Blessings from the Father flow
Her husband and family are also blessed
Her relationships you can see and know.

She and her family have put Jesus first
Jesus says, "To love Me more than these,
If you don't, you're not worthy of Me."
For I gave and you're to give
From your abundant tree.

Day in and day out
She does work for her family
Jesus says, "What you do for the sake of others
You do also unto me."

In Genesis, God gave man a helper
God knew he would need some help
A woman He created as a help to him
To be what marriage is all about.

This union will glorify the Father
But God would have to do some tweaks
For them to know the commands He gave
Must be adhered to from week to week.

The man puts his trust in her
And gives thanks to the Father above
What an amazing union is this
Sealed with the gift of love.

The godly woman is never idle
Always doing something with her hands
Being prepared for the days ahead
And for her children yet to come.

She will go through her pregnancy
Feelings as new as they were to Eve
With the pain experienced with conception
What bad feelings have come upon me.

But with the birth of her new child
Pain and sorrow are left behind
They have been replaced with a joy
That's been gifted from the divine

What is a virtuous woman
Who has taken on many things
To be subject to the will of God
Strength and honor are her clothing.

When before her savior, she stands
To hear His words of comfort to be,
"Well done, my good and faithful servant
All you've done has even been to Me."

Also to the poor and needy
She sees what must be done
To reach out and do what she can
To help the well-being of every man.

What is virtuous woman?
Your word can help to detect
The beautiful traits of a woman
With a man you've made to connect.

I Can Only Believe

When I think back of all you've done for me
That, in fact, I'm still alive
The many times I could have died
Your message to me, "You've been revived."

When you let me know you wanted me
I don't know why that you would
It gave me hope for me and my family
I can only believe because you could.

When I needed a refuge to come to
Your door has always been open for me
You've never left or forsaken me
The gift of you spirit has made me free.

Most of my day, I think of you
And the thoughts you give me to write
The satisfaction I get when I share you
Feeling your presence even in the night.

There's nothing can shake my faith
Having no faith in me but in you
You are enough whenever whatever
The gates of hell can have no effect, no, never.

The day I can see you clearly
You'll lift me up and love me dearly
All of your words will come to pass
Your love for me and my family will forever last
I can only believe.

I'm So Real

When I started My ministry
And walked upon the earth
The multitudes overwhelmed Me
They found Me in their search.

They heard that I came to heal
To release those from evil spells
And to even feed all the people
By My miracle, you all know well.

I want to be with the people
Who are looking up to Me
I care for them and am able
To do all for their earthly needs.

And more much more than this
I want to bring them to My home
Their souls are what I'm looking for
To stop that they would roam.

For I have a gift to impart
To all that would freely come
I gave Myself upon the cross
To pay for all and not just some.

Your sins I took upon Me
To pay your debt to My Father
You can have the weight of sin
Removed forever after.

I want you to get to know Me
I'm so real for you to see
Can anyone do what I have done
Remove your sins and set you free?

There's nothing I wouldn't do
That I wouldn't do for you
You can reach with open arms
My are arms are open wide

And you will know My embrace
It's a feeling you'll want to keep
To take and share with everyone
I want everyone to be My sheep.

You will know I will never leave you
You mean far too much to Me
As a shepherd cares for his sheep
I'll watch over you, and I don't sleep.

To keep you in my father's fold
I've been tasked to watch over you
Forever you will be safe and sound
I'm glad My realness you have found.

My realness is not just for here
It's for everyone, everywhere
You will know deep inside
My great love for you, and that I care.

For all to know, I'm so real
I am the real deal
There is no other: Jesus.

A Hard Nut to Crack (Paul)

"A hard nut to crack," a saying used most often
To change from what you thought was right
To something different from another angle of sight
A light gone on in your thinking
Experiencing a newness inside.

Paul was the most unlikely to choose.
A nut that was hard and hardened for years
He was ignorant of what he has to lose
His life and soul to the cavern below
Instead of new life, he would be Satan's refuge.

Paul would be Jesus's best choice
To totally glorify of who He is
A chosen vessel, he would be
In touching many lives for eternity
A new creation, he became.

We, of the hard-nut category,
Can speak volumes of our allegory
How Christ came in and changed us
Into our lives, we placed Him first
He said, "If you come to me, you'll never thirst."

We'll be fulfilled by what He gives
Most importantly, it would be His love
And everything you will need
He's constantly watching from above
To go forth and plant His seeds of love.

From a hard nut to crack
We've been transformed to something else
Our hard-nut cover we thought was safe
Has been replaced by the Father's grace
To be made new and thankful for it.

There is no nut that Christ can't crack
You who think why He would ever want me?
Remember Paul and who he was?
He became Christ's forever employee
To set many captives free.

A nut comes always from a seed
The seeds we plant have no controversy
They will grow to God's will
Jesus will always be our backer
And behold, He's the best nutcracker
Are you a nut that needs to be cracked?

If God Is for Us

Acts 5:12–42

Many signs and wonders were performed
Among the people who thought of them highly
For the apostles' connection to the Lord
Enable and empowered by Your word
To make a difference everlasting.

The lame could walk; the deaf could hear
The blind were made able to see
And the demon-possessed were freed
With all the commotion to the leader's ears
They thought action must come quickly.

The high priest rose up and captured them
To the common prison, they would go
Telling them not to teach or preach
In the name of Jesus, their King
The apostles knowing Jesus would do something.

At night an angel of the Lord
Opened the doors and let them out
Saying, "Go make a stand in the temple"
Telling who and what Jesus is all about
Emboldened by the spirit.

The apostles did early enter the temple
To speak words for all to know
That Jesus came to sacrifice
His life for so many others
That when this life is over to heaven, they would go.

The high priest not knowing they were free
Sending his people to bring them in
When at the prison, the alarm went out
The apostles were gone and teaching
How could you do anything but to grin.

The priest would somehow figure out
God was at work to accomplish His will
Gamaliel's council of what might be
Decisions were made to beat them
Then to set them free.

The priest would declare again
Not to teach or preach in Jesus's name
The apostles reply came most boldly
"We ought to obey God rather than men
For in Him is life we strive for only."

"You intend to bring this man's blood on us"
Then the apostles answered the high priest
"Jesus you murdered and hung on a tree
God has raised Him up to be on His right hand
And all judgments are at His command."

Those accusations made them furious
Their intention was to kill them
Gamaliel's advice made them curious
If God is with them, then who are we
To fight against Almighty God.

The apostles were free to go
After they were beaten and were told
Not to speak for the name of Jesus
Covering their backs was the reason
Not to lose face among the people.

Daily in the temple the apostles spoke
Preaching Jesus among the people
Rejoicing in their sufferings
Knowing what Jesus did for them.
Embracing the shame for His name.
And God is for us.

Unstrung and Undone

Words unstrung, undone; Christ will rearrange
He will give you the desires of your heart
Our King's desires will surely never change
With the giving of the Spirit, we are forever tamed.

Jesus will tune us to be most exact
To make music for all to hear
Words of our music souls to absorb
Words most precious forever stored

The Master Potter saying He is done
People seeing us as His creation
He's put us together not to be undone
And it's because of our relation

Christ has given us the tools we need
Treasures from His word is most secure
Will keep us on the straight and narrow
Experienced His joy forever more.

Falter and Fall

Dear Father, as we pass our days
Our minds going from this and that
How amazing we don't include You more
It's no wonder we falter and fall.

For us to be who You want us to be
We leave no openings for the enemy
We need to walk Your walk and talk Your talk
To have the effect that's pleasing to You.

For us to go out every day unarmed
To face the battles surely to come
How stupid to think that we will win
When we've done nothing to let You in.

For without You, we are nothing
And with You, we are everything
The gates of hell will have no effect
Against whoever You choose to select

To promote Your kingdom here and now
That all the observers will be deeply wowed.
To see God's soldiers claim victory
From what in the world can come against.

If our Almighty God is for us
Assuredly nothing can come against
The saints who are in God's army
Will have victory against all that resist.

Can there be a coming together
Of the lost so desperate for Him
That later, we call the resisters
Our most blessed brothers and sisters.

If we keep ourselves ever close to You
For there to be less instances to falter and fall
Even though we think we are close to you
This message does include us all.

Those That Wait on You

Isaiah 40:31

We are to be the waiters and servers
To the most important VIP ever
That comes through our doors to make His home
Among us with ties that can't be severed.

Jesus, when you made the statement,
"To be great be a servant of all"
For us to be your servant to many
Will be our protection from the fall.

To serve You, Lord, and then go out
For lives to be gathered for You
To step across the threshold of faith
And to embrace the miracles You do.

Each of our lives is a miracle
When we look back on where we were
We were lost and desperate for You
The great physician had the cure.

We were made whole by Your indwelling
Your spirit came to live in our hearts
Empowered by Your prayer for us
To deflect the evil one's darts.

Your desire is for us to wait on You
In more ways than the limit of time
That we will be Your waiters and servers
I'm thankful and grateful I call You mine.

And what a tip we will receive
To renew our strength by Your command
We'll mount up with wings like eagles
Not getting tired because we can

Call on You to bring us home
We aren't weary or faint of heart
Your mighty word, we have stood on
What we've depended on from the start.

Will We Be Here When We Are Gone

Will be here when we are gone
It's a question I've pondered on
With the blessed memories on earth
How many did we leave, and what's their worth.

Will memories be allowed to go with us?
Because of your forgiveness, what's left behind?
All the sinful and vengeful won't be allowed
In the Kingdom of the Most Perfect King.

I know you care about our thoughts
And our thoughts are to be about You
All the people for the short time we've been here
You've allowed us to love that are so near.

We've prayed and lifted their lives to You
So that in heaven, we will be as one
Part of your growing family
Standing before You, You say, "Well done."

I can't imagine when life's ties are cut
The people in heaven we want to see
I pray by Your grace we're allowed
To grow in our relationships still somehow

No sadness in heaven is allowed
As we contemplate family lost
I can only imagine Your love for them
For You, Lord Jesus, have paid the cost.

That all Your creation will bow to You
To acknowledge Your goodness and grace
We all must stand alone before You
To answer for our lives in life's race.

Our present thoughts of memories saved
How different will they later be?
Will there be room in my head at all?
Or will all my thoughts be turned to thee?

Relationships are so hard to sever
With our whole lives committed to each other
When our time to leave is here,
Can we let go of all we hold so dear?

Will we be around when we are gone
As I've pondered and pondered on
Where will our loved ones go with eternity lurking?
Your word and spirit will answer our searching.

Will we be around when we are gone
I don' know, and I may never
We must depend on God's wisdom and love
And His unsearchable treasures from above.

About the Author

John Sadler was an average guy from childhood to adulthood. He was an average student, a football player, a pole vaulter in track, and an average gymnast. He was an average soldier in the army. On July 29, 1979, God wanted him to stop being average and to become born into his family. "It's now or never." From the Holy Spirit in my living room was the event to where God reached down to all the way to where I was. Jesus became the author of the rest of his life story.

Married to Connie, his Proverbs 31:10 wife, daughter Bethany and her four children Michael, Lydia, Naomi and Petra, and Jonathan his son.